Cover & Interior Design by: Jodi Costa
Cover & Interior Illustrations by: Kelly Hennessy
Photography: Sisters Sweet Photography &
                 Brittany Pannebaker

Printed in the United States of America

TABLE OF CONTENTS

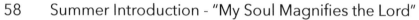

DEDICATION

Griffin:

You are my steady, my heart's home, and my favorite person of all.

I love you, Darlin'.

Harper, Paisley and Skyler:

I didn't lose myself when I became a mother,

I found myself.

You are a breath of fresh air and my greatest gift.

Thank you for making me a mother. I love you.

ACKNOWLEDGMENTS

Thank you, Tom, for giving me a space to create this book and for helping me take myself seriously.

Thank you, Jodi, for your creativity and hard work. You are incredibly talented and beautiful inside and out.

Kelly Hennessey, thank you for making my book beautiful to look at! You are crazy talented! You were able to take all of the pictures in my head and make them come to life.

To Kim Roper. Thank you for your editing skills and being okay with all of my fragments.

And to these incredible women: April, Bethany, Megan, Nina, Jessica and Jennifer; thank you for believing in me, praying for me, and encouraging me in the calling God has on my life. To have you in my corner cheering me on means everything.

Introduction

I will never forget what He showed me. It's just like God to reveal something when you aren't looking. We were in the Carolinas, and I snuck downstairs while the house was still quiet. I made myself a cup of coffee and I slowly cracked open the door just enough for me to slide through but not enough to make the hinge squeak. I couldn't risk waking up one of my sleeping babes, I just needed a moment. One quiet still moment to breathe in the morning air. The navy blue quilt was wrapped around my shoulders and I held my mug close to my lips. I sat down on the white distressed bench and I looked out at the woods.

"Do you see it?" I heard God whisper to me.

"See what?"

"The trees." He said.

"Yes, I see them. But they are just sticks, no fruit, no life, it's cold."

"Yet they are standing. And look how far you can see. You can see all the way to the other side. When you can't see anything, I see everything. Even the darkest days can show you the way."

And isn't that it? Isn't that life, our journey, our calling as a mother?

I had no idea what I was getting into when I became a mother, I don't think any of us do. It's incredible, it's indescribable and it's undeniably the hardest season of my life.

Every moment has this sweetness to it yet, a moment can turn sour faster than you can catch those little hands from knocking over your full cup of coffee; or taking the glass vase you love and dropping it on the tile floor. You feel like you are in slow motion, you can't protect them from rolling off the bed (only two out of the three of mine did). And you can't slow down one stage and rush through a second. No, every season has its purpose for your baby and for you. And that is what I have learned. Cycles, seasons and stages are a part of motherhood for you and your baby. With every step there comes a struggle and a success. Without teething they won't have teeth, without sleep training of some sort, they will never learn to sleep, without crawling and you daily saving their lives from putting some small object into their mouths, they won't be able to walk, and without walking and wobbling they could never run. It's you and it's me and it's our baby all rolled up into one. We have to have each season to prepare us for the next one.

Like those winter trees, they were standing strong through the frost, waiting for spring yet not giving up in the coldest time of the year. They had perspective, and we can have perspective in the winter and a harvest in the spring but to each season there is a place, and our place is to keep perspective in each one.

Before you know it, they will be grown and too big to rock, too big to kiss their boo boos. All those people are right. You know the ones that kind of drive you crazy at the store when they tell you to enjoy it because it goes all too fast. They are right you know. And if we let it go, we will miss out on all of those moments we were supposed to meet with God. This book comes from a heart of a worn out woman, a woman who longs to have each day be lived out to the last drop, to end each day no matter the amount of tears or struggles, and to know that I know that I was intentional, that I was filled with the grace of God and that I loved my babies so hard I planted seeds of Truth, because I only have so much time and I will do my best to not miss one. This book is full of mercy, because from one tired heart to another we need it. This book is full of inspiration from women in the Bible who became mothers with all different stories and backgrounds and insecurities and struggles. This book is real, raw, and vulnerable. It's my heart on paper. Writing has always been my best medicine and I hope that through sharing my hurts I can share my hope. And that you can finish each day of this study ready to look at yourself and your children through a different perspective, a different lens, a different life. Because this is a journey, and this is all about the seasons, and every season will serve the next if you keep your eyes open and your heart ready. Your journey into motherhood looks different than mine. Whether you got pregnant easily, if you had to go through the long weary process of IVF, or you miscarried, or you blessed a child and changed their life by adoption or fostering we are all here now. By God's grace we are all here together, on a team and for each other.

For the next 20 days, we will go through each season: Winter, Spring, Summer, and Fall. We will study what the scripture says, what each one brings, what each one takes and how you can flourish and be present and alive through each one. Each season is important, each one has lessons to be learned and love to be given to your children and love to be received for yourself. Don't be surprised if you go through a season for longer than four weeks, or more than once. We were made to be on God's time table for our life and not our own. This journey is not linear, but it's as rhythmic as the seasons. They come and they go. Some stay longer than others, and sometimes one can return with a cold front or a rise in humidity. So, whether you are weeding, watering, waiting, or harvesting God is longing to speak to you right where you are. May we discover together that for every season there is a purpose and if you are in the sunshine or in the coldest of days we were meant to grow all year long.

Seasons

Winter – def. The colder half of the year. Long.

Facts – The earth is closest to the sun during winter. Trees and plants don't die but they simply stop growing. Animals hibernate or migrate south. Insects prepare for winter during the fall by creating "antifreeze" so their bodies can drop temperatures easier. Some plants hold onto dead leaves for insulation or use deep snow like a blanket for protection.

I love winter days. Now, I am a Florida girl so bear with me, we don't experience a real winter, but we have a "winter". It gets in the 30s for two weeks and everyone bundles up from head to toe like it's 20 below. Yep, that us, and that's a Florida winter. Go ahead, judge us all you want, it's usually sunny by lunch time. (smiles) In the winter, most people see and feel cold, tired, lonely, exhausted, without fruit, dormant, lifeless. And if we are being completely honest here, I have felt like winter in motherhood. Sometimes my children treat me more like a maid then a mother. They can be emotionally up and down and left and right, and it can seem like all day I am just trying to catch up instead of leading them up to the Lord and I have nothing left to give them. Yes, winter is a cold time in motherhood.

If we look to the Bible we see a woman who was given a promise but then no sign of a child, no sign of motherhood. She was left confused and sad, she took matters into her own hands and she made a mess of a situation. This week as we study winter, we are going to be looking at Sarah's life and Hagar's life journey as women and as a mothers. We will look at their walk with God, their faith and the moments where they lacked faith. We will look at their life and your life and find the moments where God is seeking to speak to you through this season. So, bundle up, grab a good strong cup of coffee and let's get started.

This is Winter.

Day One : Stay Rooted

"And Sarai said to Abram, 'Behold now, the Lord has prevented me from bearing children.
Go in to my servant; it may be that I shall obtain children by her.'
And Abram listened to the voice of Sarai. So, after Abram had lived ten years
in the land of Canaan, Sarai, Abram's wife, took Hagar the Egyptian,
*her servant, and gave her to Abram her husband as a wife." **Genesis 16:2-4***

Remember my conversation with God I shared with you in the introduction? Well, it was a strong lesson, about finding perspective right where you are, even if the circumstance seems exhausting, frustrating, endless, sleepless, or hopeless. There is something about winter that allows you to see your life in the right way. There is a lesson from these trees. The reason they don't break and fall over or die from the bitter cold conditions is because their roots are so deep. So deep that they can withstand whatever winter may bring. Their roots are deep in the ground in Who made them, and in Who created them. They know their Source of life and they naturally dig as deep as they can to grasp for any nutrients because they know winter is upon them. What we see from these scriptures is that Sarah was given a promise, yet it wasn't happening on her time. She began to lose hope and decided something needed to be done so she could have a child. She took matters into her own hands. We see that she didn't really believe in the promise. **Her roots were not deep enough to sustain the waiting that HAD to happen.** Her faith was easily uprooted, and she was not sustained by the Sustainer.

Maybe you are in a season of waiting. Whether God has given you a promise or you are looking for an answer, either way you are waiting. I want to remind you that God is never late. He was not late with Sarah, and He is not late with you. Maybe the place you are in with your child is trying. They are pushing you, they are defying you. That can make you feel overwhelmed and completely undone.

I will never forget a month we had, that I thought I wouldn't survive. Literally, I remember thinking this will be the end of me. (Dramatic, I know, but at this point, I hadn't slept in three years! Let me exaggerate please!) It seemed that all of my girls needed me in the most intense way. No one was sleeping; whether it was a sickness, a nightmare, or teething I was up every hour or someone was constantly trying to climb into our bed. During the day, I would tell Paisley, "Please don't touch the stove," and like a moth to the flame she just had to touch it. Harper was realizing she was stronger than her sisters and was enjoying teasing them just enough to cause screaming. And any moment I tried to accomplish any task, my sweet baby Skyler would cling to my legs begging to be held leaving me one handed to complete any small task. I was overwhelmed, absolutely exhausted, frustrated and depleted. I had nothing to offer them, my patience was running thin, and I felt like I had completely lost myself.

In the midst of this season I began to let my feelings dictate my actions, and the moment I did, that was the moment I stepped out of alignment with God. Sarah was feeling forgotten and frustrated. So, she let her feelings dictate a very bad decision, one that haunts her for years to come.

Our feelings are meant to be indicators not dictators. God gave us our feelings and they are meant to be under His authority. Of course that is way easier said than done when your two-year-old won't stop screaming because they can't have ice cream for breakfast. Oh, my Paisley Joy, I do love you.

Maybe you feel like you are just not a patient mother or a gentle mother. Whatever that adjective is that you wish you possess, I would like you to think of it a different way. **You may not be naturally gentle, but you can be gentle by obedience. You may not be naturally patient, but you can be patient by obedience.** God gave Sarah a promise and all she had to do was be obedient and leave the results up to God. And the same goes for us.

Our feelings are meant to be indicators not dictators.[A]

What a promise of life, a future and of abundance to have a child and raise them and love them. Be obedient every day and leave the results up to God. Just know you are not alone. Just know the season will end. Maybe it's a month, or a week, or a few

A Lysa Terkurst - "Unglued"

months. God is right there, and He truly has not forgotten you even when you feel like you have forgotten yourself. He sees you, and if you have your roots deep in Him you might not be able to see the end of winter but you can see Him.

Have you ever felt like this is the reason for winter? To reveal how deep our roots really are? Because if you begin to see Him, you will begin to see truth over lies, you will begin to see the promises He has laid out for you in His word, and you will begin to see your children the way He sees them. Even more, you will see yourself the way He sees you. It is easy to feel lost in this calling, but motherhood does not define you.

Motherhood will make you and shape you, but it is simply not all of who you are.

You are a child of God, free, lovely, amazing, talented, one of a kind, and redeemed. Stay rooted and know He has His eyes on you.

RESPOND

- Where are your roots?
- Are you digging to find time to spend with the One who can fully nourish you or do you escape to the world of social media?
- Do you get lost in your negative thoughts instead of filling your mind with truth?
- What actions could you take to daily stay rooted in God?
- What is something to let go of so you can fully live today?

JOURNAL

_____

_____

_____

_____

_____

_____

Day Two : Keep Your Perspective

"And Sarai said to Abram, 'May the wrong done to me be on you!
I gave my servant to your embrace, and when she saw that she had conceived,
she looked on me with contempt. May the Lord judge between you and me!"
But Abram said to Sarai, 'Behold, your servant is in your power; do to her as you please.'
*Then Sarai dealt harshly with her, and she fled from her." **Genesis 16:5-6***

I want to share a "life hack" with you. This is something I do at the end of every month that has truly changed my perspective. The last day of each month, I sit down, and I write out all of the things I have learned in the past 30 days. These could be deep amazing truths the Lord has revealed to me, or it could be a simple lesson. I write down my breakthroughs physically, mentally, emotionally, and spiritually. I write down new facts I have learned about my children or memorable moments I had with them. I write down great conversations and dreams that were shared with my husband. It is inspiring to read all that can happen in a month. It always gives me a sense of relief,

accomplishment and it keeps my perspective heavenly. As a mom, at times it feels like everything just blends together. The days become weeks, weeks turn into months and just like that another year is over, but you are left feeling like you did the same things over and over again and you have not accomplished much; you have not gained ground.

The Lord has been convicting me of this thought: When I have a bad attitude about my season of life, what message am I sending to my family? I remember hearing the Lord whisper to me, "Don't let your attitude send a message to your children that following the Lord is a joyless journey." Whoa, isn't that a scary thought? I never want my demeanor to send that message. I would never want my harsh words or lack of self-control to affect how they see Jesus and how they respond to the Christian life.

During a hard season, a cold or fruitless season, it becomes easy to shift our focus to the problems and the exhaustion. **It's easy to start focusing on how we feel and to let those feelings take control.** I have come to realize that when we let our emotions take control we are giving up our power. And by power, I mean the power of God within us. When one of your children speaks to you in a tone (you know the one that makes you turn around quickly), if we give in to their emotions we are in a way, giving them the power in this situation.

Philippians 4:5 says, Let your gentleness be evident to all.

Sometimes verses are so hard to meditate on because they go against every part of our flesh don't they?

But we know we must keep our eyes heavenly. Filling our hearts and minds with scriptures, so that when those emotions rise up we know how to combat them.

Truth is stronger than tired eyes.

We know that we are tired now, and worn and ready to throw in the towel, but I am here to say that today matters. To take one day at a time, one hour at a time, one moment at a time, that is the win. That life isn't about the destination but the journey and these lessons are just as much a part of your journey as it is your babies.

When Sarah was given this promise, yes it was about the kingdom and the line of Isaac and that Jesus would come from this lineage to save the world, but it was also about Sarah. To believe and have faith when her circumstance was telling her that this is impossible. It was about her heart, and her ability to have faith in the waiting, in the unknown. The moment her perspective switched to her circumstance is when she made a mess of things. Her emotions took control, she said things she regretted and made decisions she wished she could take back. If only she would have kept her eyes heavenly, who knows how she could have experienced her heavenly Father in this time. This is your chance to experience Him while you continue to serve your family day after day. This is your moment in this hard time to find Him. He is in the waiting, He is in the storm, and He is in the winter.

RESPOND

- When worry comes, does that shift your perspective?
- How could you combat that?
- What is a scripture you can memorize and meditate on daily that will help you with your perspective?

JOURNAL

_____

_____

_____

_____

_____

_____

_____

Day Three : Stay Present

"And Sarah was listening at the tent door behind him. Now Abraham and Sarah were old, advanced in years. The way of the woman ceased to be with Sarah. So, Sarah laughed to herself..." **Genesis 10:10-12**

Sarah couldn't believe the promise that was given to her. She only could see her circumstances, her current season of life. I mean, could you imagine being pregnant at 90 years old? It was hard enough in my 20's and giving birth! No way! Here is a woman who is tired, worn out, and had always longed to have a child. But she had come to grips with it just not happening for her. She hears God give her husband a promise. And she laughs. Now? You think now is the best time? I can barely walk, and you want me to push a baby out? No way, not going to happen.

Today's topic is a personal one for me. It is my hardest daily challenge. I am always so inspired by my friends who simply walk briskly through life, who take the time to stop and smell the roses, literally and figuratively, to enjoy the moments with their

children and to embrace the day. Me? I rush. I rush to finish my to-do list. I rush when I drive. Efficiency is best and multi-tasking? I am the queen. I am determined and disciplined, which is a strength, but it is also my greatest weakness. And this is something the Lord is convicting me of. What do I choose, a puzzle with Harper or clean the dishes? Do I let them watch one more episode of Daniel Tiger so I can clean the bathrooms, or do we stop and go for a walk? I rush in the shower. I rush when I am walking. I rush when I am eating. You should see me at dinner. I inhale my food before Griffin even sits down. He will ask me how it tastes and I'll say something like, "I have no idea I didn't think about that." Or, "I just eat because I have to and I eat before I have to share or someone needs me."

Oh, but if only I would slow down and enjoy my life, my kids, my husband, myself. How different would my life look? It might be a little messier, but I would be truly living it, and I would be fully in the present instead of striving for perfection. What am I rushing for and where am I rushing to?

The Lord has been opening my eyes to this truth that I rush because I think I have something to prove. I rush because I think it will be better once I complete this, or things will get better once I get to this place. I'm sure a lot of us can agree. Especially in our social media world where everyone is posting the best of the best, photoshopping and cropping, using the best filters; it's easy to feel like you are missing out or that your life is just a little shy of everyone else. Your home will never look like theirs, your body will never be that perfect, and your children will never be like that. The rushing leads to comparison and the comparison leads to discontentment. Suddenly you are longing for a different home, different body, different hair, different season or even more a completely different life. I think we were all better off before smart phones and social media. But that is a subject for another book.

... we must fight to be present ...

What I am trying to say is that for your children, your husband, yourself and God, we must fight to be present. There is so much in this very moment that we will miss if we are too busy rushing or looking ahead. Sarah couldn't see the promise in the present season and she let fear take over. She laughed at God and thought "what good could come out of this?" Dear mama, so much good can come out of your darkest and coldest day if you choose to stay present and in pursuit of Him. **The past has become a part of us; the future is unknown to us but today...today is a gift to us. That is why it is called the present. Do you live like it is a gift?** [B]

RESPOND

- What is something that you need to let go of to help you stop rushing?
- What is a way you can pursue God right in the midst of this?
- List five good things about this present season. I know they are there, you just have to choose to see them and not the circumstance.

19

[B] Ann Voskamp, The Broken Way

JOURNAL

_____

_____

_____

_____

_____

_____

_____

_____

_____

_____

_____

Day Four : Choose Joy

"And Sarah said, 'God has made laughter for me; everyone who hears will laugh over me.'" **Genesis 21:6**

"She (Hagar) gave this name to the Lord who spoke to her: 'You are the God who sees me,' for she said, 'I have now seen the One who sees me." **Genesis 16:13**

Choosing Joy - this is one of those things that is easier said than done. Those two words have become a cliché in today's Christian culture, but let's take some time to dig a bit deeper into the truth that lies underneath this small sentence. To "choose"- that is what the Lord has given us - the freedom to choose. It is a powerful thing. It is everything. Every day we wake up with the ability to choose. We choose what to wear, we choose the food we eat, we choose what to do and we choose how our attitude will be. A choice.

Webster defines choose as "to pick out or select (something or someone) as being

the best or most appropriate of two or more alternatives." Every day we choose what we think is best for us, for our family and for our spouse. If you are truly in a winter season choosing the best option, the one that you know is best for your soul, can seem like a mountain to climb. Sometimes we get so drained from serving and pouring out that we feel lost, we feel empty, we feel unnoticed. Just like in our story, Hagar fled from Sarah but God met her there, in her darkness, in her winter. And she named that place *"For you are the God who sees me," Genesis 16:13*. And He sees you. He sees your faithfulness, He sees you trying, He sees your love, He sees your heart and your weariness, and He sees and knows how much you are in need of Him.

I have found many ways to help me choose joy, but I don't want to tell you what to do. I simply want to open up a space for you to think, create, and be inspired; but, if I may, I would like to share two ideas. One of the biggest things I have learned through motherhood is that I must really get to know myself. Who I am and who I am not. Through these tiny little people I am raising, the Lord has used them to rock me to my core. He has broken walls down, He has pruned, broken chains, and re-shifted my focus time and time again. I wouldn't have been able to receive any of that correction if I wasn't willing to choose it, to be open to it.

Here are two simple ways I choose joy:

1. I have a thankful journal. Since I married my husband I started writing down all of the gifts, the big and little moments, the people, the laughter, the good cries, the hard lessons or the "sunshine after the rain" if you will, and the places I am thankful for. They range from Griffin's perfect blue eyes to the smell of coffee brewing in the morning. From getting into a bed with fresh sheets to the way Skyler wraps her arms around my neck and plays with my hair, it's all in there. And those are all little moments that I CHOSE joy. And because of those little moments, they have added up to one big sigh of relief, one big exhale. This season is hard, lonely, tiring, selfless, but look … look at the gifts in the midst of the season. Look at the joy that can be found when I choose to see it. Get a journal and start writing. Your gifts are all right there.

2. I get in the Word. I know you have heard that before, but I would love to really share what I do. Many times, just like you I only have five minutes to myself, but I sneak away and I get into the Word. I first ask the Holy Spirit to reveal truth to me through the Word. Because the Bible is alive, and I know with the Spirit's direction He will lead me to the right place. I study the Old Testament a lot. I love reading about the lives of those who have gone before us. It's amazing, and I encourage you to do that. Opening up to the Psalms will encourage you to worship and praise. Worshipping in gratitude has the power to change your attitude. Reading the letters will give you direction for the day. But the thing is, when you choose to fill your mind with the Word of God it will never leave you empty. It will always satisfy. Netflix and social media are empty. And if we are honest, they usually leave you feeling discontent and that you are not good enough. So, when you choose to fill your mind with the Truth, the only result is feeling refreshed, loved, and joyful.

Worshipping in gratitude has the power to change your attitude.

Sarah was blessed with a gift, which based off of her attitude she didn't deserve. Her lack of faith, her rushing to make things happen, even her ugliness didn't stop God. So even if today you can look back and see times where you made the wrong choice or your emotions got the best of you, it doesn't matter, there is grace and God wants to bless you. When Sarah received what her heart had been longing for she laughed, joy overcame her, and she was amazed at what God had done. If you don't have your promise yet, even if it is still hard, choose joy, choose to laugh and worship God. Because worry ends when worship begins. We serve a God who is waiting to bless you, meet you where you are and love you today.

Worry ends when worship begins

RESPOND

- What are five things you are thankful for?
- Look at your daily schedule and make time every day, even if it is only five minutes, to spend time in the Word.

JOURNAL

_____

_____

_____

_____

_____

_____

_____

_____

_____

_____

_____

_____

Day Five : Cling to Hope

"Then God opened her eyes and she saw a well of water. So, she went and filled the skin with water and gave the boy a drink." **Genesis 21:19**

We often forget Who we have on our side, don't we? It is so easy to get completely overwhelmed by our circumstance, our situation, and our daily grind that we forget God is for us. We are not walking alone and the impossible can REALLY be made possible with God. If we give God our best He has something to bless. [C] I love that thought. We can only control so much. But we can easily feel so out of control as a mom. I remember one day, Harper was playing with every single toy we had. And we are conservative, so I thought we surely don't have a lot, but when everything is out at once and we are playing castle and everyone is a princess, it took over the playroom and her bedroom with a choo choo train ride from one to the other. Meanwhile, my sweet Paisley, God bless her little heart, couldn't stop spilling. She kept missing her mouth, dropping her cup, and just having one of the clumsiest mornings of her entire life, and then my baby started throwing up. What was going on in the Gilstrap household?! I hadn't had coffee, I was on day three of dirty hair, praise the Lord above for dry shampoo, and no matter what I did I couldn't get ahead of the messes, I couldn't control the morning and I couldn't stop the madness from continuing. Everyone was mad, or sick, or sad; it was

[C] Havilah Cunnington's Podcast "Havilah's Podcast"

a lot of emotions, tears, and playing and then tripping over toys because there were too many out. I was constantly saying, "Oh, that's okay, sweetie" or "don't worry, Mommy can clean it up, we will try again." Yet with every spill my tone got sharper and sharper and my voice got louder and louder. Can't you just see it? Total disaster. And completely out of control.

The idea of remembering that God is on our side, and if the best I can do in that situation was to kiss boo-boos and clean up spills and whatever else was coming at me (or on me) then I could have made it through. But instead, I shamed myself. If only I washed their hands more, Sky baby probably wouldn't have caught the stomach bug that is going around. If I was just as attentive with my second child as my first then she would be better skilled with her utensils and for the love of it all, she probably wouldn't be spilling so much. I also said things to myself like, "I bet Griffin is having an awesome morning. Quiet ride in the car to work, talking to adults, enjoying his warm cup of Joe that probably has never had to be microwaved once, or twice, or three times!!!" Like where did Griffin come in and why am I resenting him? It takes two to make a baby! But again, I have lost sight, lost perspective and am trying to control and when we try to control we forget the freeing feeling we were created to live in.

He is for you and He has you right where He wants you.

What a freeing feeling it was when I truly owned that. I cannot control it all, I can only do my best in this tiny moment, this morning, this car ride, this time out temper tantrum, and the rest or the results I should say, are up to the Lord. If I believe He is who He is, that He brought me to this point, why would He ever stop providing and leading and guiding and loving? He would never. It is not His nature, it is not who He is. So as a mom, you can only do so much in 24-hours, so why do we always try to fit in more? Or why do we think we need to? God only wanted 24 hours in a day; He knew we needed rest, sleep, and quiet. He knew our work would be hard, our mothering would be weary, incredible and a beautiful calling, but He also knew He would be the only source of true refreshment.

There is only so much you can do for your children. You can plant seeds of truth, love and the gospel. You can teach them how to be kind, that they are made in the image of God, that they are beautiful, strong, and free. But then … then you must take a deep breath and trust in the Creator who created them. He loves them more than you, which doesn't even seem possible, but it is!

We see Hagar as she had lost all hope. She saw her life as completely falling apart. She didn't ask for this and now she has hit the end. She is out of control. But God, in His reckless love, shows up and provides just what they need for the moment. He gave her a well of water which was a sign of hope from the Lord that they would be okay.

Today, cling to hope, because you will be okay too. If you feel lost and alone as a mom, cling to hope. If you feel weary and worn, cling to hope. We have hope on our side, and we have God right with us. There is freedom and peace and strength when we live in that truth. In this winter season, cling to hope because He has much to teach you in the here and now, and He has so much love to pour onto you.

RESPOND

- Find someone in your life that can hold you accountable and encourage you to remember the hope you have in Jesus.
- What are three things that the Lord has revealed to you through this season?
- What are three ways that you have grown through this season?

JOURNAL

Spring - def. Originate or arise from. Symbol of rebirth.

Facts - The first day of Spring means "new day". Increased light, more exercise, and more skin influence hormonal levels. Children actually grow the fastest in springtime.

    I was researching Hannah, and according to BibleGateway.com, Hannah is the woman who personifies ideal motherhood. That is quite the title. Her name alone means "gracious and favor." She is a woman of unblemished character yet she walks through sorrow, a deep sorrow that many women have had to face. We will talk about that but mainly we will talk about what she did in the midst of the sorrow; she prayed and she sought the Lord. Her response was worship, songs, praises to God and a promise to keep. Even though she is not in the Bible for very long, her chapters stand out to me as a woman to aspire to. Her character, her inner beauty, and her reverence for the Lord are just a few of the characteristics I see in her. I can't wait to share them with you.

Spring: a time of the year many cannot wait for. It comes right after winter, the things that once fell asleep begin to wake up. Cold days turn warm, soaking into sun thirsty skin. And everywhere you look white blankets melt into bursts of color. A feeling of refreshment, life, newness, and revival flood through hearts. And in motherhood, spring is the season to worship and to plant seeds of truth for your children's souls and also yours. To break habits, find rhythms and move forward. I have much to share with you in the next five days.

This is Spring.

Spring

Day One : Contentment

"But to Hannah he gave a double portion, because he loved her,
though the Lord had closed her womb." 1 Samuel 1:5

Hannah's story is full of grace, which isn't too surprising; her name means grace. But her journey doesn't start out beautiful, it starts out broken. The Lord has closed her womb. Why? Why would the Lord close her womb? She is clearly an amazing woman. She goes to the temple to worship every single day, she honored God, and feared Him. She respected her husband, and in turn, her husband loved her deeply and gave her double portion. He felt sorry for her and longed for her to be happy. She clearly was a woman of honor, and she would be an amazing mother. So why did the Lord choose to close her womb? We will try to unravel this question over the next few days, but what I want to focus on is during the hard season, the time of not having what her heart truly desires, she is content. Yes, she still felt sad, she cried, she was at times so overwhelmed by the hurt in her heart she would not eat. Yet … she kept going to the temple. She kept worshipping God; she never stopped praying. She found her hope when it all felt hopeless.

She found her peace in the Prince of Peace and she learned to be content.

In Psalm 16 it says, "The boundary lines have fallen for me and they fall on beautiful places." I love this thought because it is essentially saying, "I accept God and the boundary lines He has put on my life." Whether that refers to your house, your finances, your children, your relational status or your occupation, you have found contentment and you believe that they fall on beautiful places. You trust God in this season. What power, what strength and what peace Hannah has. This shows me that her identity was not wrapped up in whether she was a mother or not. We can clearly see that this was the desire of her heart, but her identity was found in the Lord.

So, when I think of you, I want to remind you that your success and your identity is not based on your motherhood. Our role as mothers is to train our children in the way they should go. And to see those correction moments not as disruptions, but as a moment that God is letting you see the state of your child's heart. Turn that moment into an opportunity to call out the wrong, and to teach what is right in a loving, kind, and gently way. Our contentment is not on the success of our children, or the behavior of our children.

We cannot change them, only Jesus can, that is why He came.

That is spring, isn't it? The discipline to take care of the garden every day because you know the harvest will come. The flowers will bloom but you must be content right where you are in doing this side of the work; the dirty work, the hard work, the work unseen. It's the most important work. Do you have a four-year-old that knows enough to think they know it all and is questioning your every decision? Nurture those questions. Teach Godly principles out of love so that second-hand faith becomes first-hand. Do you have a toddler who truly defines the term "terrible twos" that on a daily basis there is more crying than laughter? Their emotions are a roller coaster and you are running on the track just trying to catch up. (Not like I am speaking from personal experience or anything.) Be patient. Teach patience. How many times have I caved in to my feelings and yelled or slammed a door? In the moments where you can't be patient or calm, remove yourself. Trust that the Lord will give you another opportunity to show love and self-control tomorrow.

The way to teach contentment is to be content. Be vulnerable with God in those places. He has been trying to get your attention in those places He wants you to become content. Maybe it is the season of life where you are in the constant selflessness and putting the needs of another before yourself. Maybe it's your post-baby body or your finances. Maybe it's that you are getting older, whatever it might be. Be real. Be raw.

And be honest with God. I promise He will fill those places with love, and once they are filled, contentment comes.

Because, contentment is a soul thing, a spiritual thing.

No natural part of you will have it or want it. Contentment is digging the dirt up to drop the seeds down so that strong roots can grow.

RESPOND

- Are you struggling in a certain area of your life to believe the boundary lines that God has marked have fallen on beautiful places?
- Is your child or one of your children pushing you? How could you take the time to teach them contentment and show them love today?

JOURNAL

_____

_____

_____

_____

_____

_____

_____

_____

_____

_____

_____

Day Two : Pray Before the Day

"As she continued praying before the Lord, Eli observed her mouth.

Hannah was speaking in her heart; only her lips moved, and her voice was not heard.

Therefore, Eli took her to be a drunken woman.

And Eli said to her, 'How long will you go on being drunk?

Put your wine away from you.'

But Hannah answered, 'No, my lord, I am a woman troubled in spirit. I have drunk

neither wine nor strong drink, but I have been pouring out my soul before the Lord.

Do not regard your servant as a worthless woman,

for all along I have been speaking out of my great anxiety and vexation.'

Then Eli answered, 'Go in peace, and the God of Israel grant your petition

that you have made to him.'

And she said, 'Let your servant find favor in your eyes.'

Then the woman went her way and ate, and her face was no longer sad."

1 Samuel 1:12-18

 One thing I have experienced in my life is the power of prayer. My life changed dramatically when my father left us when I was fourteen years old. My world fell apart and we went into survival mode. It was just me, my mom, and my older brother. And we had to start all over and

figure out how to do this. I had to grow up fast and my mom took everything upon her shoulders to give my brother and I a great life. She was amazing. She was strong, brave and such a fighter for us. But there were times when we did not have the money for food. And my mom would find a check for $200 in our mailbox from an anonymous person. Random?

Random doesn't exist in God's world.

No way. My mom needed help paying for our tuition and she would go to pay it only to be told that someone paid for our year of school. This happened over and over again in my life. God, just showing up.

When we found out we were expecting our second child, we were very surprised. The way I found out I was pregnant was truly crazy. Just imagine going to get an ultrasound making sure a cyst on your ovary was gone only to find out your six-week-old baby was looking great! I am sorry, my what? That's my uterus? Yes, you want to hear the heartbeat? You mean my heartbeat? I am sorry…WHAT? Yeah … it was nuts, but amazing … but that's a story for another time. Anyway, Griffin and I were not prepared for this wonderful surprise. We did not have the financial means to handle another child, no gear for two babies, we didn't have another crib or a second car seat. We didn't have the space or the tools needed. But I tell you what, in seven days, we found $500 under our doormat, two people gave me two different kinds of double strollers for free and someone else gave me a free crib. No one knew I was even pregnant. All I did was pray.

Prayer is a gift you know. It's an amazing moment that you have to capture the attention of our Creator and share your heart, your dreams, your fears, your needs; to pour out praise, to worship before the miracle, to honor and to adore Him. And yes, I am one of those crazy people who believes you can pray for anything. I mean, why not? He loves us so much; I think He loves when we simply talk to Him. He already knows what is on our minds, and He already knows what we need and what we want.

He loves us so much that often He won't give us what we want because He knows it's not what we need.

So here we find our girl. Hannah is depressed, heartbroken, hopeless, exhausted, weary in soul and being tormented by Peninnah. [Read 1 Samuel 1:6-7] She is crying out to God. She is open, raw, real, vulnerable and she is going on and on for so long that people are noticing her. They assume she is drunk because of her intense passion and endurance in prayer. She is praying fervently. She is promising God, she is laying it all down. And when she is done, it says her face is no longer sad. No miracle had come yet; she wasn't pregnant. What she wanted had not been given to her, but her face, her countenance, her inner being changed.

You see, when we pray we feel hopeful, refreshed, alive, okay, undone to be remade, broken to be made whole.

We start faithless and we end faithFULL.

It is who He is. When you spend any time in His presence, you can't help but to change. We are soul beings, and even though Hannah's circumstance didn't change, her soul did. For all she knew, she would never have a child, but she had hope because God reached out and filled her up. Just like in Spring, you plant seeds having an idea of what should happen, but the outcome is not in your hands. You actually take the seeds out of your hands, out of your grip of control, let them go, and plant them into the ground hoping life comes out. **And you can be sure with God, there is only abundance; never lack, never half empty only filled to the brim kind of love.**

I think as believers we often times forget to pray. Before you walk into the room and you don't know what to say to your child who is just pushing every button and inching themselves over the line … pray. Before you get out of bed, pray. Before you discipline, pray. Before you make decisions, pray. The atmosphere will change in your heart. And "out of the overflow of the heart the mouth speaks." Your circumstance might not. Your children won't suddenly stop fighting, but you will have the wisdom to know how to handle it. Your morning might not get easier, but you will have the patience to help set a joyful tone in your household so this day starts out right. Your baby might not miraculously start sleeping through the night, but you better believe He will miraculously give you the strength to get up and comfort them every time they need you. And when you get sleep it will be sweet. [Read Proverbs 3:24]

You see, when we pray, all that we gain trickles down into our motherhood which then pours into the cups of our children. We will sprinkle the fruit of the Spirit on them - it's contagious. We are their inner voice, we teach them how to pray, how to love, how to be kind, how to give, and how to be patient. Can you believe their world view is being shaped right now? Let's pray today. Make this day count.

RESPOND

- If you honestly look at your prayer life, is it where you want it to be?
- Is there something or someone you feel called to pray or even fast over?
- How can you teach your children about prayer today?

JOURNAL

_____

_____

_____

_____

_____

_____

_____

_____

_____

_____

_____

Day Three : Plant Seeds for the Harvest

"Samuel was ministering before the Lord, a boy clothed with a linen ephod. And his mother used to make for him a little robe." 1 Samuel 2:18-19a

Here we have our girl, and she finally recieved her heart's desire! What I love about this part of Hannah's story is how clearly you see that Hannah instilled truth in Samuel the moment she held him. Can't you just see it? She is speaking truth over him, the love of God over him. She is teaching him how to worship, how to honor God, respect God and fear God. She had knit him a small tempeh (the proper attire for men when entering the temple of God) so when they went to the temple Samuel would be dressed appropriately before he even knew what he was wearing. She was planting seeds. Hannah's time with Samuel was so precious. She knew it would come to an end sooner than she wanted. [Read 1 Samuel 1:11] So, she made every day count, and she planted deeps seeds of truth in him.

In the springtime, seeds are planted, land is plowed, watered, maintained, and taken care of. It's a chance to nurture those little things because you know if you do this part well, the harvest will be full. If the seeds are nurtured, watered, and given light there will be fullness of leaves, their roots will be strong and if they are planted in the right place, no matter what comes, the tree will stand. Do you see what I am getting at? It's springtime.

45

Even in the fall or summer, it's always spring in their hearts.

Everyone always says to me and I am sure you too, "Wow how fast they grow." Or, "Enjoy it while they are little because it will be gone before you know it." And how cliché but oh how true. My youngest is inching closer and closer to two years old, and I am trying to soak up every single minute of the last bit of baby I see in her. Of how small she is, her wonder of the world around her, her little feet, her dimples on her knuckles, her little voice as she is learning new words and how every time she says it right she smiles and claps for herself and waits for me to join in the celebration of one more thing she has learned. But often it feels like sand running through my fingers; I just can't slow it down. **The days are long but the years are short, and every day is a true chance to plant those seeds in their hearts.**

Every day is a chance to plant seeds to tell your child who they are in Christ, to

explain to them the awesomeness of God from the power of God to the details of God. To tell them how wide, high and deep the love of Jesus is for them. The time is now. Every night I sing, "Jesus Loves Me" over Skyler. I didn't do this with the other two; the Spirit led me to do this while I was in the hospital with her. I remember, I was lying on the bed cuddling next to her. This was my third baby but I had never delivered at a hospital before so it was very different for me. Griffin had just left to go home and be with Harper and Paisley and it was just Sky-baby and me. Her tiny hands, her perfect features, I will never forget it. I just met her, but I felt like I had known her my whole life. I sang her that simple song. And I have sung it to her every night before I lay her down to sleep.

Maybe she needs it, maybe it's a declaration over her life, but that simple song is truth. She is loved by Jesus and she belongs to Jesus. Those two truths alone can define a person's life, can't they? Start now. Even if they are five and you feel like you just missed the boat. Start today. Maybe they are much older, and it seems impossible to start right now. Get up and go tell them truth. Our voice will become their inner voice.

Telling someone who they truly are in Christ is power to break any lie the enemy attempts to whisper.

You have the power to do that; they're your seeds to plant.

RESPOND

- How do you feel you are doing with speaking truth over yourself?
- What is something that you feel your child needs to hear?
- What is one way you can have the atmosphere of your home be more like Hannah's?

JOURNAL

_____

_____

_____

_____

_____

_____

Day Four : Savor the Sacrifice

"She left her baby, Samuel, at the temple of the Lord and left him to serve there all the days of his life." **1 Samuel 1:11**

I know a woman. She has two children and one on the way. She has a loving husband who is doing his best to provide for his growing family. He has dreams and is longing to be at a higher position in his career, but he has to work very hard to get there. She has dreams, and every day she lays them down to pursue her assignment right now, which is to raise these sweet little boys. All her time, her energy, mentally, physically, and emotionally goes to these boys. Her body is growing bigger as her third little boy grows and is nourished, fed and full. Literally her organs and bones are moving and being pushed to the side for this baby to grow. She has been uprooted from her family that she has been surrounded by for support and love all of her life. She packed up everything and moved to stand by her husband and his dreams. They have moved thousands of miles away from all that they have ever known. She gave it all up - all

the comforts, the house, the family right down the road. She gave up the familiar church family, her father the pastor, the beach and the waves for the Chicago skyline, the sunshine state for the windy city. She changed it all for her husband, for her boys, and their future. She has sacrificed and continues to sacrifice. And her heart; it's soft, ready to receive from the Lord. Her mind is strong and focused on the promises of God that He is faithful, that

He finishes what He starts and that no word from Him will ever return void.

And God is proud of her, in love with her and is blessing her. This is my best friend, and watching her walk through this past year has been inspiring.

I'm sure you can think of women in your life who have sacrificed. Maybe it's your mother, a friend, a grandmother, or maybe it's you. Honestly, we all have sacrificed. Motherhood is the ultimate sacrifice. It's this constant connection to the cross, to the laying down of one's self every single day for the sake of others. It's putting others needs before your own, it's praying and teaching and pruning. It's wiping little buns and countertops every day. Its loading everything into the car only to unload it all back at home. It's teaching how to tie shoes and use the potty. (I think now I will forever call it a potty) It's teaching the gift of sharing, and reminding them of the gift to share. It's disciplining, even when it hurts you more than them, and it's being consistent for them every single day.

No one really tells you how hard it will be. No one tells you the exhaustion you feel mentally, that there are truly some mornings you just don't want to do it, any of it. No one tells you that you will never sleep again! But even if they did, would it have really changed your mind? Would it have stopped you? No way. (And maybe they did tell us, we just don't listen. I'm glad I didn't.) Think of Hannah. She pleaded with God to give her a child. She longed for that sweet moment of a baby being placed in her arms, and she was faithful and believed and when God blessed her, she did the ultimate sacrifice. She held true to her word, and when it was time, she gave Samuel to the temple to serve for all of his life. ALL OF HIS LIFE. She didn't get to wake him up, she didn't get to make him breakfast, teach him, play with him, raise him. She gave him away, just as she promised. I don't know how I would have gone through with it. That moment of letting him go, of kissing him one last time. But she did, and she did it joyfully! She praised God! Come on girl, couldn't you have complained a tiny bit to make me feel better, and be a little more like us? No. Not Hannah. She praised God for the blessing, for the time she had with Samuel, and she thanked Him for His sovereignty. And then she says this prophetic truth that some scholars believe goes beyond King David all the way to the birth of Jesus. 1 Samuel 2:10 says, "He gives power to his king, he increases the strength of his anointed one."

I don't want you to miss this. Scholars have studied this; commentaries have been written about this one verse that say she is really speaking about Jesus. She was in this state of servitude and sacrifice. She had such strength in her faith in God that not only did she do as she promised by giving her one and only son to the temple, but the posture of her heart was of praise. She was so connected to the Holy Spirit that she spoke prophetic words over her son Samuel who would anoint King David, who is in the lineage of Jesus Christ! Oh to be like Hannah.

Her sacrifice played a significant role in her son's life and in the coming of our Savior.

Let's be in a place with the Spirit that no matter the constant sacrifice, we can surrender and serve with a heart that savors every step.

Because what we are doing now will affect generations to come.

RESPOND

- How has your attitude been with motherhood? Where could it be better? Be honest.
- Are you feeling connected with the Spirit? If so, where has there been fruit of that? If not, how could you find time to reconnect?
- When you think of the word sacrifice, who comes to your mind and why?

JOURNAL

_____

_____

_____

_____

_____

_____

_____

_____

_____

_____

_____

Day Five : Count Your Blessings

"So it went on year by year.
As often as she went up to the house of the Lord…"
1 Samuel 1:7a

Hannah was not the first woman recorded in the Bible to walk through infertility, she was the fourth. First it was Sarah, then Rachel and then Rebekah. But what is different about Hannah's journey is that she walked through those years with unwavering faith. She believed in God's promise with her whole heart. The other three? Not so much. Sarah laughed mockingly when she heard God talking to Abraham. (Genesis 18:12) Rebekah questioned. (Genesis 25:22) Rachel ignored the responsibility of believing and seeking God. She pushed everything aside in her mind and heart. (Genesis 30:1) How easy it is in moments of trial and suffering to laugh and think, "Yeah right like that will really ever happen for me." Or to doubt … goodness we all doubt, it's an instinct for me sometimes. Or how many of us just push aside the feelings, try to cover it up, and stay busy so we don't think about it. Suppress the pain and wish it away. But here we have Hannah. She was facing one of the most heartbreaking seasons of her life. I have many women in my life that are walking this journey. I personally did not experience this, so I won't even try to explain the pain. It's indescribable, unable to be grasped in words and paper, but it is gripped by God and covered in His mercy and grace. You can just picture Hannah, month after month, holding her breath and the blood flows instead. Yet, she prays, she cries out, and weeps before the Lord.

She comes face to face with the pain WITH Jesus and He overwhelms her with peace.

And where does she land? On solid ground knowing His word does not return void. She might not always be standing strong; sometimes I bet she crawled to the temple, dragging her feet because the hurt was so strong. But she landed on the truth, in the truth.

And you know what … she had five more children after she dedicated Samuel to the Lord! I am smiling as I write this. In 1 Samuel 2:21, it says she had two daughters and three boys while Samuel grew up in the presence of the Lord. That's five more children, and the number five biblically means grace. How fitting. God didn't just honor Eli's prayers for Hannah, but he continued to bless her! What a full life! You see, I believe the way we get through those dark seasons is by counting the gifts. They are there; sometimes we have to open our eyes to really see them. And when we get through the dark season, spring is always around the corner. That's the perspective we must have. Winter will come, yes, but spring is right there. All of creation knows it, and so must your heart. He is faithful. He knows your needs and your wants. He will see you through. It might look different than you ever imagined: it might not end in your dreams coming true, but the result is not up to us nor can we tamper with it. Our part is the walking, the crawling, the running through: the obedience. It's having faith. **"Faith is the space between what you once knew and what you know to be true."** [D] I love this thought because faith is is not knowing the outcome, it's the letting go of the state of mind that wasn't really getting us anywhere, and it wasn't helping us get better. It was familiar, yes. Comfortable? Maybe. But was it best? No. **Not all good things are God things**, and that's where faith comes and keeps your eyes on what you know to be true. The promise, the dream, the kingdom, JESUS!

So, wherever you are today, I want to encourage you to count your blessings. You cannot worship and worry at the same time, lay it all down at the feet of Jesus and breathe in deep breaths of promise and faith knowing that He sees you, He knows what you need, and He will see you through.

RESPOND

- Does your perspective often shift to the problem or the promise?
- How can you find time in your day to worship God and find a Kingdom perspective?

[D] Havilah Cunnington's Podcast "Havilah's Podcast"

JOURNAL

_____

_____

_____

_____

_____

_____

_____

_____

_____

_____

_____

Summer - def. The warmest season of the year. The days are long, and the nights are short. It can stand for draught, hottest temperatures, and discomfort.

Facts - The root word of summer is Sem which means together. Some of the most colorful and vibrant flowers bloom in the summer. Most animals have their babies in the spring so that they can raise them in the summer when the food is plentiful and there is safety in numbers. Trees fight for sunlight by bending and growing in different directions to get as much of the sun as they can.

Summer brings family time, relaxation, hot days and cool nights. It can bring moments of simplicity of just being together and making memories, and family vacations and no school which creates more time to bond and play and learn and grow. Yet on the other hand it can also mean drought, exhaustion, patience running thin and mental weariness setting in. The desire for the schedule and the pattern of school to begin can be all that we want. Just like the earth it is all about the sun ... the Son. If we are not fixated on getting as much of the Son as we can, then just like the trees, we won't survive. Summer, can be about growth and depth and love, but we must make time to be exposed to the Son and drink up the Living Water. Then and only then can we flourish.

This season is a tricky one. It has not come easy to me to write about. I have actually been putting it off for a few weeks. What I have come to realize is that this season is good and bad. It is split right down the middle. You can thrive in the summer, in the midst of the long days, the hot, the hurt, the broken. It is all a matter of what you magnify. You can also completely melt away. You can be lost in the lies, the pain, the weariness, and the change. We are going to look at a woman this week, a woman who was used as a trick. No one wanted her, she was judged by her looks. She was not valued, and she was in competition with her sister whether she wanted to be or not. She struggled at first. Complaining, falling apart in the battle, the weariness, but by the end of her story, she finds God. She finds hope and she chooses to praise the Lord, so much so that it changes the whole way she sees her children! We have so much we can learn from Leah. I am very excited to jump into this story with you.

This is Summer.

Day One : What Do You Magnify?

"Tell me what shall your wages be? Now Laban had two daughters.
The name of the older was Leah, and the name of the young was Rachel.
Leah's eyes were weak, but Rachel was beautiful in form and appearance.
Jacob loved Rachel. And he said,
"I will serve you seven years for your younger daughter Rachel."
Genesis 29:15b-18

Leah's name means "weary". Whether that refers to her heart or her lack of beauty, either way, she was weary. Regardless, the Bible is clear in stating that Rachel was clearly "better" than her. She comes into our story and is quickly compared to her sister. Rachel is more beautiful than her and more desirable. The only reason Leah married Jacob was out of a lie, complete deception. He didn't want her … no one wanted her. She believed lies that she was not good enough. Unloved. Not worthy. She believed she would never meet the standards of her culture. She wasn't valued, wasn't seen, and she was alone. That is all too close to home for me. Having a father who left, my worth was shattered. I felt not good enough to love. My identity was all over the place and I began to search and seek for my worth in all the wrong places instead of pursuing the One who gave me my worth. Have you ever felt this way?

If you carry any of these lies in your heart, it's time to speak a new word, a new name, and my goal for this week is to break lies that you have believed about yourself and for you to see what God has planted in your heart from the very beginning. Our culture is all about competition. There is a race and if we are not aware we are going to jump in and start running in it and we are going to lose. The social media standard of a perfect life is a lie. Deception of beauty is everywhere. It's hiding on every magazine shelf and in every photo. The standard of beauty changes, the "goals" are unsustainable. First, it's a big chest, now it's big backsides, thigh gaps, full lips and eyebrows that are on fleek (whatever that means). Leah doesn't need to meet the standard and neither do we. This week, we are going to draw attention, highlight, and bring forward all the truth God placed in your heart from the moment you were born.

Griffin was in the bathroom getting ready for work one morning and Harper, who was three at the time, was sitting on the countertop just looking at herself. She turns to Griffin and says, "Daddy, I love me!" What a profound statement from a three-year-old. She looked into the mirror and was pleased, not just pleased but delighted in what she saw! She saw beauty, brown eyes, a cute nose and a big smile. She loved the way her crazy curls fell across her face and every which way. She loves how her smile is so big, her eyes squint, and her head always tilts to the side. I don't want that to change, oh my heart's cry is to guard that for her.

When is the last time you looked in the mirror and were delighted? You were happy with what you saw? The truth is, our children watch how we look at ourselves and they will imitate what we do and how we respond. You might feel like Leah today and simply feel weary. The sun is hot and the days are long and you are done. It's been a rough morning or a long week and you feel like you can't do this anymore. You look in the mirror and childbearing and child raising has changed your skin, your eyes, your hair and you are unhappy with that. And you know what, that's fair. I am right there with you.

But if you are comparing and competing and trying to keep up, you are running the wrong race.

Focus on the truth and beauty that God wrote on your soul and let that dictate how you look at yourself, your circumstance and your motherhood. It's time to call yourself by a new name.

RESPOND

- What lies have you believed about yourself?
- Identity, that is a strong word. Take a moment and think about where your identity is. Write down your thoughts.
- During the day, what do you magnify? The negative or the positive? Why?

JOURNAL

_____

_____

_____

_____

_____

_____

_____

Day Two : Continue

"So Jacob served seven years for Rachel,
and they seemed to him but a few days because of the love he had for her."
Genesis 29:20

Sometimes our circumstance is broken. Sometimes the season we are in is draining us completely. Sometimes we can become so wrapped up in our circumstance that we forget one of the biggest truths.

God doesn't look at our life in seconds, He looks at it in seasons.

We are a people that count the seconds. We need things fast and we need things now; Amazon prime, binge watching a show, and drive-thrus. We don't want to wait, we don't want to have to be still, we are impatient, compulsive, and irrational at times because we forget to see life the way God does. We forget that He made seasons, and He created the world to function that way. Look at the trees, look at the tide. There is a rhythmic timing to it all. This place you are in right now, just like summer, it might be hot, tiring, long, and intense. But if we can say to ourselves, "It is only a season, and God will see me through, "we can continue. Continue with hope, with confidence, with grace and with endurance.

The season Leah was in was long, hard, and broken. She was unloved by her husband, despised by her sister and felt as if she had no purpose or calling. But she continued. The Lord saw her, the Lord loved her and she stayed present in that. It didn't mean she danced around and was happy and ignored the situation, but the posture of her heart was of praise ... even if the praise was ugly, broken and filled with tears.

Motherhood can break you but God wants it to make you.

We cannot base our success off our children and their obedience. Now is the season of continuing. It's the moment you hear them fighting in their room ... you whisper to God, "If I go in there right now, I will not handle this well. Please give me another chance tomorrow." Sometimes that is the best thing we can do. Before you walk into a room and lose it, stop, breathe, and pray. The Holy Spirit is willing and waiting to give you the words. You are already filled with the fruits of the Spirit, you just need to tap into them. So today, continue. Don't strive to do something grand, just be. You are doing a good job Mama. And today you can't fix it all. **But tomorrow is the fruit of what you sow today, so take it slow and continue.**

RESPOND

- How can you make your load lighter today?
- What is something you can do before you get to your breaking point with your children?
- Find a place in your house where you can "retreat" to even if it is for a moment to calm and collect yourself. Where did you pick and why?

JOURNAL

_____

_____

_____

_____

_____

_____

_____

Day Three : You Have Favor

"When the Lord saw that Leah was hated, he opened her womb." **Genesis 29:31**

Leah became pregnant and gave birth to a son. She named him Reuben, for she said,
"It is becasue the LORD has seen my misery.
Surely my husband will love me now." **Genesis 29:32**

Having favor means being shown kindness or goodwill far beyond what is expected. This is how God sees us. Sometimes this comes in material blessings but it is usually spiritual. In this case, Leah first found favor with the Lord opening her womb. But that didn't change the state of her heart. She was blessed with children but she was still broken and she was living in that brokenness.

God can give us favor but we can miss the gift. [E]

Leah needed God to meet her right where she was. She thought having children would solve her problems, that it would replace the pain. And I think we do that. "If only I could have this house, then I will be content."

E David Raegan, "Favor of God", 2001-2018

"If only I could get married, if only I could have these clothes, this couch, this pair of shoes, this car, then I will be happy. I won't ask for anything else." I am guilty of this. **But what I have come to understand is that nothing on earth can satisfy the God-sized hole in my soul.** We weren't created for this world. The Bible says we are simply passing through. (Hebrews 11:13-16) So why do we get wrapped up thinking that material possessions will fill us? This is a topic that has been written on and preached on countless times, but that's because it is so true and it is becoming a bigger issue.

Our world screams at us all the things we "need". And if we are not careful, we let those voices drown out the Voice. Our children are forming their worldview right now. How to treat people, how to share, what happens when they get in trouble, how to love others, and what to expect! What choices they should make when it comes to food and what Christmas will look like. What is it all about? How many presents will I get on my birthday? Is life really about me getting or is it about God and giving?

There is a beautiful favor on your life. It's not in things you can grasp but it is in spiritual blessings. Freedom. Peace. Love. Joy. Trust. Hope. Forgiveness. Redemption. I spent time with a woman the other day. She was inviting. She was beautiful. She lit up a room when she walked in. She loved on others. When you spoke she listened attentively. She was quiet and loud all at the same time. She walked with purpose and with grace. She was inspiring. She was the most beautiful woman I had ever been with. She was 83 years old. Her husband had passed away and she was living alone. She didn't have much, she didn't need much, but she had it all. Her beauty came from within and she loved Jesus. She had peace, she had joy, she had hope. And when I was around her

I could breathe. I felt invited and wanted. I felt loved and valued. She lives her life knowing she has favor from the Lord and she changed my life. I don't know about you but that is the kind of woman and mother I want to be. One that lets my children be who they are and tells them that who they are is good. A mother that makes them feel invited, wanted, beautiful and valued. It starts with your heart and your awareness that you have found favor in the Lord.

RESPOND

- Count your spiritual gifts today. Where do you have favor?
- What kind of woman do you want to be? How do you want to make people feel when they are around you?
- What is a material possession that you need to let go of?

JOURNAL

_____

_____

_____

_____

_____

_____

_____

_____

_____

_____

_____

Day Four : Comparison Traps

"When Rachel saw that she bore Jacob no children…" Genesis 30:1

"When Leah saw that she had ceased bearing children…" Genesis 30:9

We all do this, don't we? We look at what someone else has, and what we don't have and we feel jealous. Suddenly, our lives are not complete without it. We can't stop thinking about it and our everyday, ordinary life seems empty until we have it. Like when we get it, whatever it is, it will change us, make us, and fulfill us. Comparison is that dangerous sneaky trap the enemy likes to lay at our feet all covered up so we can't see it. Like leaves over a hunter's hole, we are being hunted for our contentment, our peace of mind. It was the first lie in the garden. The snake made Eve to think she needed something she didn't have. This led to discontentment, and this led to the fall of man.

Discontentment changes everything. It did in the garden and it will change everything in your life. The moment we believe the lie that God is withholding something from you out of spite, or anger, or that He doesn't love you, doesn't know what's best for you, everything will unravel. Did you catch the word in the verses I shared today? The same word is in both sentences. It is the word "saw". Rachel and Leah couldn't be more different, yet they both only saw what they didn't have. They didn't see all the good, the gifts and the blessings that were in their lives; they only could see what they lacked. Isn't that just like us? I have felt that so many times. We get caught up in the loss, in the need, in the wants. We see someone else's life and all of a sudden we compare ourselves, and if our lives don't look like theirs then we must be going too slow, we must be incomplete, and what we have is not enough. We can do this with our houses, our children, our husbands, our post-baby bodies, our possessions, our path in life, all of it, any of it. The danger lies in what we choose to see. What we see affects our decisions. Our decisions dictate our life. Our life determines the state of our souls. I love the scripture in 3 John. Verse two says, "Beloved, I pray that all may go well with you and that you may be in good health, as it goes well with your soul."

We can only be well if our soul is well.

We can only be content if we believe and trust God. The inside of us flows to the outside. When your soul is well, your health, your thoughts, your sleep, your actions, your words, will all be well. We are loved by a God who doesn't withhold unless there is a purpose and a plan. The purpose and plan has a place in the calling on your life. Be aware of the traps of comparison, they are always covered up but never too big to jump over.

RESPOND

- What is something that causes you to compare? Is it a certain person on social media? A show? My challenge for you today is to remove it. Unfollow, block, hide whatever it is, and track how you feel without it in your life.

- If you could rate the health of your soul on a scale of 1-10, where would you be? Why?

- What are you choosing to see? What you have? Or what you lack? How could you improve or change this?

JOURNAL

_____

_____

_____

_____

_____

_____

_____

_____

_____

_____

Day Five : The Mundane Matters

"And when all the flocks were gathered there, the shepherds would
roll the stone from the mouth of the well and water the sheep,
and put the stone back in its place over the mouth of the well."

Genesis 29:3

If you think about our lives, 80% of our days are boring. (I know, how encouraging does this sound? Trust me, keep reading.) It's true though, isn't it? Especially as moms we get in a pattern with our children. Same thing, same story, same daily routine, and it can begin to wear us down. We can begin to feel weary in the midst of the mundane. I do think it is good to break the pattern and go on a spontaneous adventure. (I like those days but only when they are totally planned out perfectly in advance by me but spontaneous surprises for my children.) But I want to talk about the mundane, the 80% of our lives, because God gave me a breakthrough in this. And now my 80% feels different, it has weight and value and it has shifted my perspective. God has revealed to me that

how we handle the mundane
sets us up for how we will
handle the spiritual moments.

The Webster definition of mundane is "of this earthly world, rather than a heavenly or spiritual one." The world's duties are described as mundane and they are separated from the spiritual realm, but what God is showing me is that He is in the mundane. I always saw them as separate. Hurry up and get the dishes done, fold the laundry, etc so then I can have time with the Lord, then I can have a heavenly moment. But why can't I experience God while I fold my husband's shirts? Because I'm pretty sure God is with me the entire time, and He is waiting for me to turn my eyes and ears to Him. And the more we can take control of the mundane in our lives, the more detailed and caring we can be for that 80%, and the more prepared we will be for a spiritual encounter in the midst of the mundane and in preparation for the extraordinary moments that God puts in our lives. The ones where He is going to use us, bless us, speak through us.

The mundane matters. We must take ownership and do every detail well and set ourselves up for success. You know that piece of the game that has been sitting on the edge of the counter for a week that you just don't feel like going and getting the game down and putting it away? You know that shirt that has been in the laundry room "air drying" that you need to put in your closet? The toys, socks and shoes that are in your car that you need to sort and put away? It's all those things. If we can learn to do those well, to take control of those little mundane tasks, then we will feel a shift and feel a change in our days.

Our scripture for today sets the scene for Jacob and Rachel meeting. There was a schedule the people lived by and because of their timeliness and consistancy in the "not so fun" parts of the day, God's plan took place. We see in this scripture how the sheep were taken care of. The stone protected the well, and it had to be put back after the sheep were given water. All the shepherds in the land brought their sheep to this well. There was a process to the little things and this little process led Jacob to meet Rachel, because they were doing the mundane as shepherds and a shepherdess. And because they did the mundane well, they met, fell in love, and the lineage of Jesus continued. Don't you see?

The mundane can make room for miracles and the mundane can prepare you for your purpose.

RESPOND

- Is your mundane draining you? What is something spontaneous you can plan for you and for your family?
- What is something you can add to help you manage the mundane? Maybe a basket at the bottom of the stairs you collect things in all day and take up at night? A bag in your car you fill up and empty on Saturdays? Is it a system for your kids with what to do with their shoes and backpacks right when they get home?
- How do you feel like the Lord is preparing you for your future in the midst of your mundane?

JOURNAL

_____

_____

_____

_____

_____

_____

_____

_____

_____

_____

_____

Fall – def. A period of maturity.

Facts – *Fall marks the transition between summer and into winter when the days grow shorter and the leaves start to fall. The plants use sunlight to keep their green color, so as the sun grows less and less during the fall, the leaves start showing a different color. Yellow and red sit below the green all the time, they just only come out during the weakening of the sunshine.*

Wow, can you believe that? The colors are always there. The bright yellows and reds, they stay under the green all the time, it's just only visible when the sunshine is no longer so bright, when the days grow shorter and the period of maturity has come. Therein lies this shedding process, the letting go of the old, the broken, not walking in the pain, lies, or rejection anymore. Not living in the labels of the past, the hurts, the hang ups, but letting the true beautiful colors shine through. They have always been there. We try to cover them up by something we think will be best, but really everyone loves the fall. Everyone loves the leaves, the colors, the differences, the feeling that fall brings. We can't capture it enough in pictures and paintings. And to think it was always there all along.

Uncertainty scares us. When we are unfamiliar with the way a road winds around the trees and you cannot see past the long bridge, you are tempted to doubt. We want to see point B when we are standing at point A. And that is simply not the case, that's not how it works, that's not how God works. Each day is filled with choices to make - big and small. Every decision carries weight, even in the ones that seem insignificant. These moments are not meant to bring out our own abilities, but they are meant to reveal where our trust and confidence lies. So as we look at fall, be at rest just like the fields knowing Who supplies throughout the seasons. Even the seasons where things slow down, decisions must be made, and we don't know what the future holds. Let's study how the Father provides through it all.

This is Fall.

Day One : Breathe

"Then Pharaoh commanded all his people, 'Every son that is born to the Hebrews you shall cast into the Nile, but you shall let every daughter live.'" **Exodus 1:22**

Jochebed is pregnant with her third child. Miriam was her oldest, they believe around 10 years old and Aaron was about 3. She heard the news that Pharaoh was coming to kill all the baby boys, to be thrown into the crocodile infested Nile River. Can you imagine her angst? Her worry if she was having a boy, she didn't know yet. I can't imagine how afraid I would be. Should I run away? Should I go somewhere to hide? If it's a boy, how would I keep him safe? We as mothers face countless questions. Will my baby be healthy? Should I vaccinate or not? Should I do day care? Stay home? What

food should I buy for her? What if I can't breastfeed? What if we can't get into the school we want, what if the baby rolls over in his sleep and can't breathe? Are these clothes too big? Will they get tangled up in them? Too tight and she will suffocate? What if they can't walk? What if they aren't smart? What if? What if? What if?

If we focus on the unknowns, fear will run our minds, won't it? Psalms 29:11 tells us, "The Lord gives strength to his people, he blesses his people with peace."

I believe we pray all wrong sometimes. We are asking for peace, patience and self-control, but the thing is we already have it in Jesus. Ephesians 1:3 says, "Blessed be the God and Father our Lord Jesus Christ, who has blessed us in Christ with every spiritual blessing." We already have these gifts, yet we struggle because we are not always connecting with the Holy Spirit. Ephesians 4:30 says, "And do not grieve the Holy Spirit." Sometimes I believe we do that by not tapping into the power we have in Him. We are the home of the Holy Spirit and we need to claim that. We miss it because we focus on our limitations instead of God's unlimited blessings. We have the power to cast out fear, lies, and brokenness. We have the power to defeat the "what ifs" that will run rampant in our thoughts. What I love about Jochebed is that she didn't run, she didn't rush ahead or try to do something out of her anxiousness. She was still. And deep in her heart she trusted God. [F] Jochebed's name means "the honor of God" or "to God's glory." Her life was for the glory of God, so she knew no matter the outcome, it was all to honor Him. See the key for us as moms is to learn that

... God isn't in the rushing ...

the hurrying, the worrying, the anxious thoughts. **He is more in the delighting (Psalm**

[F] "Bible Gateway: All the Women of the Bible"
https://www.biblegateway.com/resources/all-women-bible/Jochebed

37:4), the abiding (John 15:4), and the dwelling (Psalm 91:1). That's where He lives. And if we live there, those fears flee in the presence of peace, in the presence of truth. Fear has no place. Lies have no place. Rejection has no place.

As we begin this week together, whatever you are facing, whatever is in your future, choose to delight yourself in the Lord. Abide in Him and dwell in the shelter of the Most High.

RESPOND

- What is a place you can claim peace over in your life?
- Is there something in your future that instead of worrying about you can dwell in His presence?
- What is a way you can honor God in your motherhood?

JOURNAL

_____

_____

_____

_____

_____

_____

_____

_____

_____

_____

_____

Day Two : Embrace Change

"When the child grew older, she brought him to Pharaoh's daughter,
and he became her son.
She named him Moses, 'Because,' she said,
'I drew him out of the water. Exodus 2:10

I am one of those strange people that really loves change. (Don't judge me.) I don't ever want to get too comfortable I guess. Or maybe it is just the free spirit in me, but I am always up for trying new things. I love getting a new type of phone so I have something new to learn. I can never order the same thing at restaurants, even if I loved what I got the last time. Every time my husband leaves for a trip, I find a way to change something on him. Ask him how many times I have moved the silverware drawer, he just loves it. (wink) **And what I also love about change is that ... God never does.** You know what you will always get with Him, and it is everything we need. Faithfulness, love that never ends, forgiveness, grace, mercy, hope and a future. He is totally and utterly reliable. And

in a world that is constantly changing - the beauty standard, the new trends, the level of fame or success - God never changes. And that is why I believe we can embrace the changes that come here on earth.

Without change we cannot grow.

Think about it. The soil breaks so that the seed can be planted. The seed breaks open to produce a flower, to produce beauty, a moment to breathe in the sweet fragrance of His love and faithfulness. And it all happened because of change. As mothers we must be able to change and adapt. The moment you have your two-month-old figured out they are six months old and then you must learn a new way, a new schedule, and a new daily routine. Oh, the beauty of a baby who doesn't move can be a season we often look over! But mamas, relish the fact that you can put your baby on the bed and they don't move! If I am totally honest, all of my children fell off of our bed. When our first born fell, I cried and truly thought I killed her but when the second and third fell I quickly scooped them up before Griffin saw and had them laughing in just a few minutes. (True story I am the more relaxed parent, possibly too relaxed.) But we must be ready for change. When Moses could not be hidden any longer, Jochebed had to do something. She knew if she kept hiding him in the house he would become too loud or too visible as he began to grow and he would be found, taken and killed. She adapted and prepared a plan the best she could. And that ability to change saved her child's life.

Sometimes as moms it is easy to get stuck in the season and avoid what is happening. Because change requires work. And work requires re-thinking the sleep schedule, retraining the steps, re-working the plan because your child is growing, and your child is needing you to adapt so they can keep becoming who they were meant to be physically, emotionally and spiritually. But on the other hand, as they change we must be able to stay the same. As they grow and experience new emotions, new places, and new developments - maybe it's a new friendship, a new school, a new environment - we have to stay the same for them. Consistent, patient, loving, and kind. We must learn the moments to push and encourage and when to be silent and let them move when they are ready. It's not easy, no, but it's necessary.

Just like when we go somewhere new and try something scary for the first time we look to God for peace, courage, and confidence. We go with the changes, but we remain their steady, their comfort. Our children look to us in the same way.

One morning I was having breakfast with the girls and Harper said, "I know I'll never find a man like Daddy!" (I know, right. My jaw dropped, too.) But she continued and said, "I love how it's the same with Daddy, I know what I am going to get when he comes home from work. A big kiss, a big hug and then he chases me."

Isn't that just like our Father? He comes down and meets us right where we are. Whether we are in a good mood, a grumpy mood or a sensitive mood. He loves on us in all the ways, He gives us hugs and kisses, and then He chases us with His love, mercy and grace. And He does it every single time. I promise you even though you don't know what will come out of your current situation,

... you know what you will always
get with God.
And it is always, always good.

RESPOND

- What is a way you need to adapt for your child today emotionally?
- What is a way you should look at this season differently with what they are going through?
- What is a way you need to stay steady and stay the same for them?

JOURNAL

_____

_____

_____

_____

_____

_____

_____

_____

_____

_____

_____

Day Three : Prepare Your Heart

"When she could hide him no longer,
she took for him a basket made of bulrushes and daubed it with bitumen and pitch.
*She put the child in it and placed it among the reeds by the river bank." **Exodus 2:3***

I woke up to screaming. And not the, "I'm scared and I want mommy to comfort me" type of screaming, but the whiny scream. The, "I'm unhappy and I am awake and someone better fix this." This happened day after day after day. Paisley went through a four-month span when she was two where she chose to wake up like this every day. I am sure something was going on in her head internally or emotionally (there is always something) but all I could see and hear was her choosing to be this way, and there was nothing I could do or say to make her happy. So, for the first hour or two every day for four months she cried, whined, asked for things then yelled at me when I gave them to her because she changed her mind. She wouldn't let Griffin touch her, so he wasn't able to help me at all. Until at some point in the morning she would suddenly be happy. Like a switch, she decided to turn that frown upside down and be joy. (She better be joy, that's her middle name, dangit!) I was not ready for that phase and I had no clue as to how to get ahead of it or how to get out of it. It's like this constant feeling of not moving fast enough or saying the right thing at the right time. Then before you know it, the whole moment has spun out of control, and there is nothing you can do to get ahead of the situation and make it better.

Everything is different in hindsight, but as I look back on that, I realize I didn't prepare my heart. Every night I would talk it over with Griffin, strategize what I could do or change. How I could speak to her and look at her with this big smile no matter what, and how that would fix it. I thought of all of these great ideas in my head, but my heart was not prepared. There is 18 inches between your mind and your heart and it is amazing how off balanced they can be. How many times I know a truth in my mind, but I don't know it in my heart.

And that is where the anxiety and stress and worry and frustration are fought ... in the heart.

A better way to have prepared myself for my little bucket of sunshine every morning would have been to prepare my heart. Prepare my heart with scripture or have worship music on in the morning. Because the truth of that situation was that I was not going to make it better. This was Paisley's problem and I was getting wrapped up in it. I needed to let her be however she needed to be, and I needed to create an environment in my heart that poured out peace, love, joy, gentleness, and self-control no matter what.

Phew … that's a lot easier said than done.

I want to talk about this scripture with you. The tools that Jochebed used to make this basket for Moses were no joke. They were real craftsmen tools, and she worked very hard through blood and sweat to make this basket strong so it could protect her son. She was going to do everything she could to give him a fighting chance of survival, and she prepared her basket like she prepared her heart. She knew the outcome looked bleak in her mind but in her heart, **in her heart she was trusting in God's unwavering faithfulness. And from the heart she built this basket, from the heart she didn't give up, and from the heart she was diligent.**

So today I want to challenge you to think about your heart and think about your mind. Where is the gap? Where is the imbalance? What is the truth that you know in your mind that you can't seem to get it to your heart? The heart is a spiritual thing, a God thing, a His timing thing. So, stay steady and keep pressing in. The breakthrough is coming.

Today prepare your heart not your mind.

RESPOND

- How do you need to prepare your heart as a mother today?
- What is a truth from the Bible you know in your mind but struggle to own in your

heart?

- What is a struggle that you are waiting for your breakthrough?

JOURNAL

_____

_____

_____

_____

_____

_____

_____

_____

_____

Day Four : Gather

"…So the girl went and called the child's mother. And Pharaoh's daughter said to her,
'Take this child away and nurse him for me.
And I will give you your wages.'" **Exodus 2:8-9**

The word "gather" in Greek is "sunago", which means to lead together, to bring together, collect, assemble or receive with hospitality.[G] And when I think of a family during fall, we are usually coming together. There is something about the break in weather, the leaves changing colors, the jackets, the sweaters, the pumpkin flavors and scents that has an essence of togetherness. Whether it is memories of your childhood or a longing of what you desire to create within your family, it feels like a time to gather.

We find our mother here having to let go of her beloved son.

To trust God, not in place of the doubt, but in the midst of the doubt

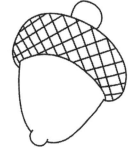

that He would guard and protect Moses, that God would see her through and see her baby through. She trusted God would be with him, even if she couldn't be. That they would come out of this season on the other side

[G] W. L Walker, https://www.biblestudytools.com/dictionary/gather/

not grieving but receiving a promise.

And God was faithful. I'm finding that He always is.

This time last year I had no job, we were living in a 1000 square foot apartment and there was no house in sight. I felt stuck. I felt like I wanted to lead my family into this season of opening our doors and "gathering" people together. From our family, from church, from old relationships to new fresh friendships, the burning in my heart to have a place for that was unquenchable. Yet it felt so far out of reach. So, in essence I had to let it go. I had to trust God with the dreams, the future and all that my heart desired and believe that we would come out on the other side opening a literal door to our very first home. And He was faithful.

I have now been in my home for nine months and have been blessed with a freelance writing job that is a big step closer to my dreams and my calling. Which is this book, this heart of mine on paper. Writing has been the best medicine for my heart and I long to help heal your wounds and mend your scars through my words. So maybe you are waiting right now. I wanted to offer an invitation that no matter what your reality looks like, no matter your home, your wardrobe, your hair that maybe hasn't been washed in three days like mine, or your skin that is looking more tired than vibrant, I want to invite you to gather. Gather your family together and serve them, love on them, and give them your time. Why? **Because Jesus always teaches us that it is so much better to give than to receive and when we give, the blessings come from heaven.** And just as Jochebed gave her son up, she then received an incredible blessing of getting him back plus being set free. He is faithful. He always is. And He always will be.

RESPOND

- What does the word gather mean to you?
- How could you show hospitality today?
- What is something you need to let go of today?

JOURNAL

_____

_____

_____

_____

_____

_____

_____

_____

_____

_____

_____

Day Five : Focus on the Unseen

"When she opened it, she saw the child, and behold, the baby was crying. She took pity on him and said, 'This is one of the Hebrew's children.'" **Exodus 2:6**

God has been teaching me something lately. It's been one of those painful processes, you know, the ones where we are going to stay uncomfortable for a while until we have been set free from a limiting mindset and healed from past lies from the enemy. And that is exactly where I am. I didn't know I had pride, I didn't know I had been seeking my purpose in all the wrong directions, and I didn't know I was looking at the wrong things.

This all came to a head when I was sitting on my floor surrounded by my three daughters ages three and under. My hands were full, the house was a mess, the circles under my eyes marked the many hours of sleepless nights, and my ability to make rational decisions was about to be all out the window. I was overwhelmed and exhausted because all that I could see was not going the way I planned. The girls were not having a good day. Let's just say I wasn't feeling like I was #winning at this whole mom thing. There weren't going to be any super cute posed Instagram pictures right now; this was real, and raw and ugly. I remember feeling this weight on my chest and thinking I cannot do this, I can't keep up at this pace. And I then remember hearing His voice say, "You need to focus on the unseen."

The light cracked through the blinds shining perfectly onto my daughter's bright blonde hair. Her curls bounced up and down as she ran to get a new book for me to read. All three of them began to crawl on me like a jungle gym fighting to sit in my lap. (Cute yes, yet slightly overwhelming for those of us who are claustrophobic.) I read the book, but my mind was dwelling on the thought of focusing on the unseen, like faith, like believing in Jesus, like having hope in the future and all that He will do that hasn't been done yet. Yes, the unseen. I took a deep breath as they all ran for the door hearing Daddy's car pulling up to the driveway. I stayed there, just sitting, thinking, how do I focus on the unseen here in this? I looked around the room at the mess, the spilled milk on the counter, the crayons that were scribbled on the white table, the crumbs from the crackers they had at lunch. And I felt the weight again. I remembered the laundry that was still in the dryer from yesterday, the smudges on the bathroom mirror that I want to clean before my mother-in-law comes over to watch the girls. The dishes that are in the sink, the dinner I still need to make. Oh, if I could turn it all off, and search for the unseen. How do I see the unseen?

And there it is, the sound of Griffin tickling them with his beard that is patchy, stubbly, and tinted red and perfect. The pitter-patter of their feet down the hall. The hall that will be in all of their childhood memories. It's Paisley singing at the top of her lungs as she runs back and forth on the couch as if it's her stage. It's Harper and how she never leaves her Daddy's side when he gets home from work. It's the memories we are making, not the mess. It's the dinners that were shared around our table, not the time spent making them. It's the way I made them feel. The unseen. That's what lasts.

Forever.

I was brushing Paisley's long hair one night and to keep her from running away I ask her questions. "What's your favorite thing about Harper? About Skyler? About Daddy?" And for every answer she said an activity they do together. And when I asked her what her favorite thing about me, She said, "The way you smell, and the way I feel when you hug me." The unseen. Take a moment and think back on a childhood memory. You might be able to see what you were doing, but more than that you remember how you felt. We have a chance every day to focus on the unseen. Those moments that will be etched in their brains, that will shape and mold their hearts and will affect the way they love others and live their life. We have this moment today and now. I challenge you to let the dishes go. What's one more day of that load of laundry sitting in the dryer and you choosing to focus on the unseen? The relationship. Stop what you are doing and look at her when she is talking to you. Play the game instead of paying the bill, chase him instead of choosing to do the dishes, because yes, those things are important, but they shouldn't control your day. Live with intention, live with purpose. You are doing kingdom work. And God wants to use you to shape your children, but He also wants to use your children to shape you.

RESPOND

- As we finish up our time together, what is one way you can focus on the unseen?
- Being intentional is so important in the midst of this busy season. Have you found a way you can be intentional with your children? Maybe it is a different way for each one depending on their personality. Write out the ways you can intentionally pursue them.
- What is something God is speaking to you? As a mother, as a woman, as a daughter and child of God. What is something He is telling you?

JOURNAL

THE AUTHOR

HEATHER LYNN GILSTRAP

Heather lives in Clearwater, Florida with her husband Griffin and their three daughters Harper, Paisley, Skyler, and a baby on the way. She is a stay-at-home mom, who serves alongside her husband ministering at Harborside Christian Church in Safety Harbor, FL. While wearing many hats, Heather continues to pursue her calling to write and speak. She co-authored her first published book "Refocus" in 2016. In her free time, she works out, reads, blogs and bakes sweet treats for her family.

You can keep up with Heather at www.heatherlynngilstrap.com

THE ILLUSTRATOR

KELLY HENNESSEY

Hi, my name is Kelly Hennessey and I am the Designer and
Owner of Hennessey Letters. I have always had "pretty"
handwriting, but when I got engaged I decided to start
working on developing that skill. I was able to design and
letter all of my own wedding decor in 2016. Pretty soon
after coming home from our honeymoon, my husband encouraged me to pursue this skill
more, and to consider selling my work. I first started an Instagram account, next came my Etsy
Shop and before I knew it I was selling at weekend markets! I love the chance to work with
clients and bring their vision to life. My projects range from home decorations, gifts, charity
items, and my favorite of all - weddings! I have really enjoyed working with Heather on this
project, and I cannot wait to see how the Lord blesses her work!

Follow my lettering journey on Facebook and Instagram @HennesseyLetters

reFocus: A Manageable Bible Reading Plan is the perfect tool to focus and/or refocus your heart, mind and soul clearly on what matters most in this life. It is a tool for you to grow in your relationship with God and in your knowledge of Scripture. reFocus enables you to move at a pace that works best for you, with three levels of reading plans-Simple, Moderate and Intense. There is plenty of space to journal your prayers and thoughts or track what you are learning as God speaks into your life make reFocus a great devotional tool.

Enjoy the journey as you reFocus and see clearly what God does in you this year.

Made in the USA
San Bernardino, CA
26 March 2019